HAVE SOME PUN

SWEAR WORD COLORING BOOK
HILARIOUS SWEARY COLORING BOOK FOR FUN AND STRESS RELIEF

FOR THE DIRTY AND DEPRAVED MIND

Outrageous Katie

Copyright © 2016 by Swear Word Coloring Book Group

ALL RIGHTS RESERVED. By purchase of this book, you have been licensed one copy for personal use only. No part of this work may be reproduced, use or redistributed in any form or by any means without prior written permission of the publisher and copyright owner.

Claim it, its FREE!

Like free stuff? So do I! Come check out the site and get yourself some freebies! Follow me IG @OutrageousKatie and Facebook!

www.outrageouskatie.com/free

Who doesn't laugh at a good dirty joke? I know I do. Each page in this book should have you either blushing or giggling like a kid. Just don't become overly 'excited' and please keep them from your small children HA!
Enjoy this book and make sure to check out my other titles, they are guarenteed to make you laugh or cry.
-Outrageous Katie

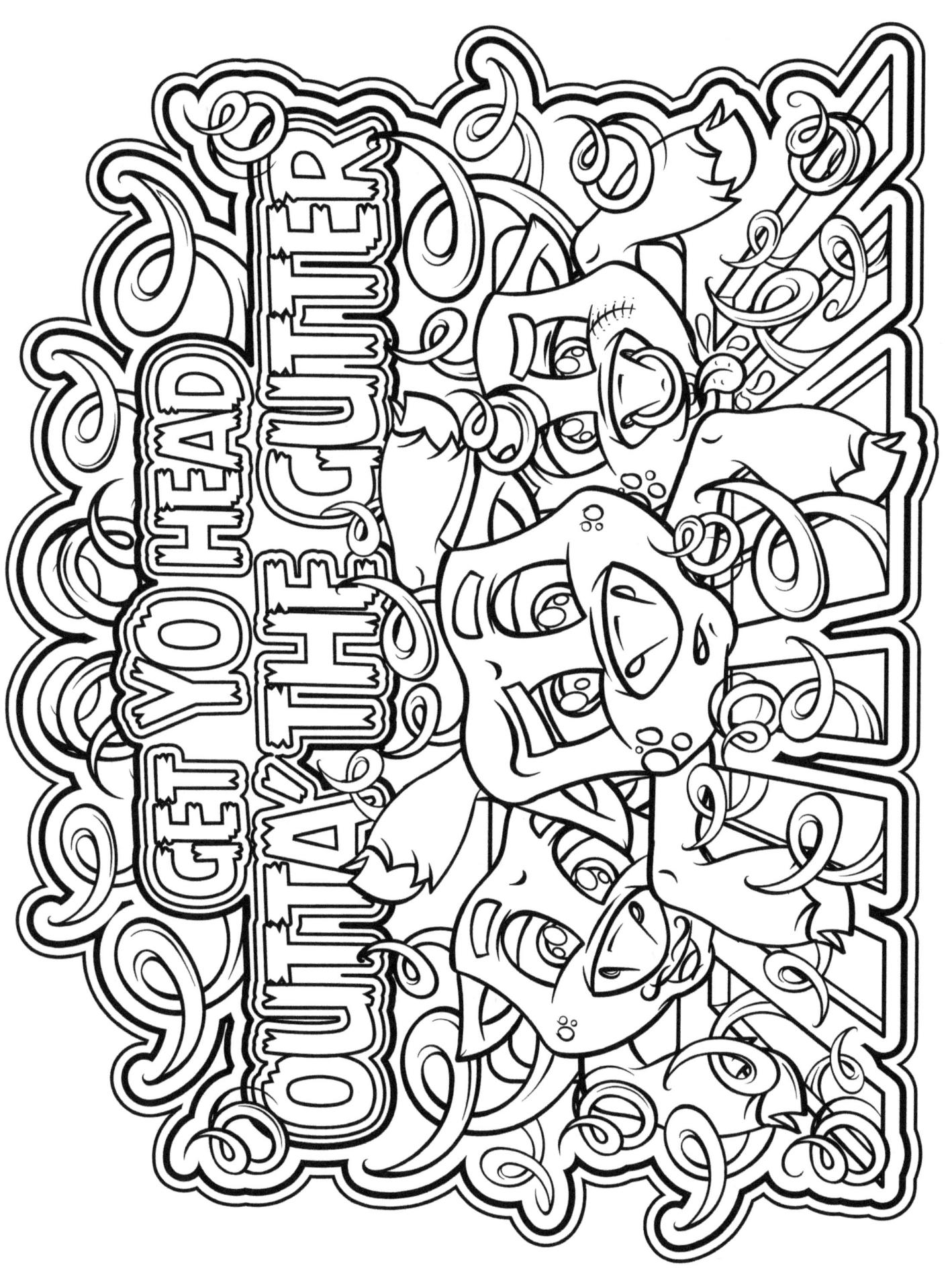

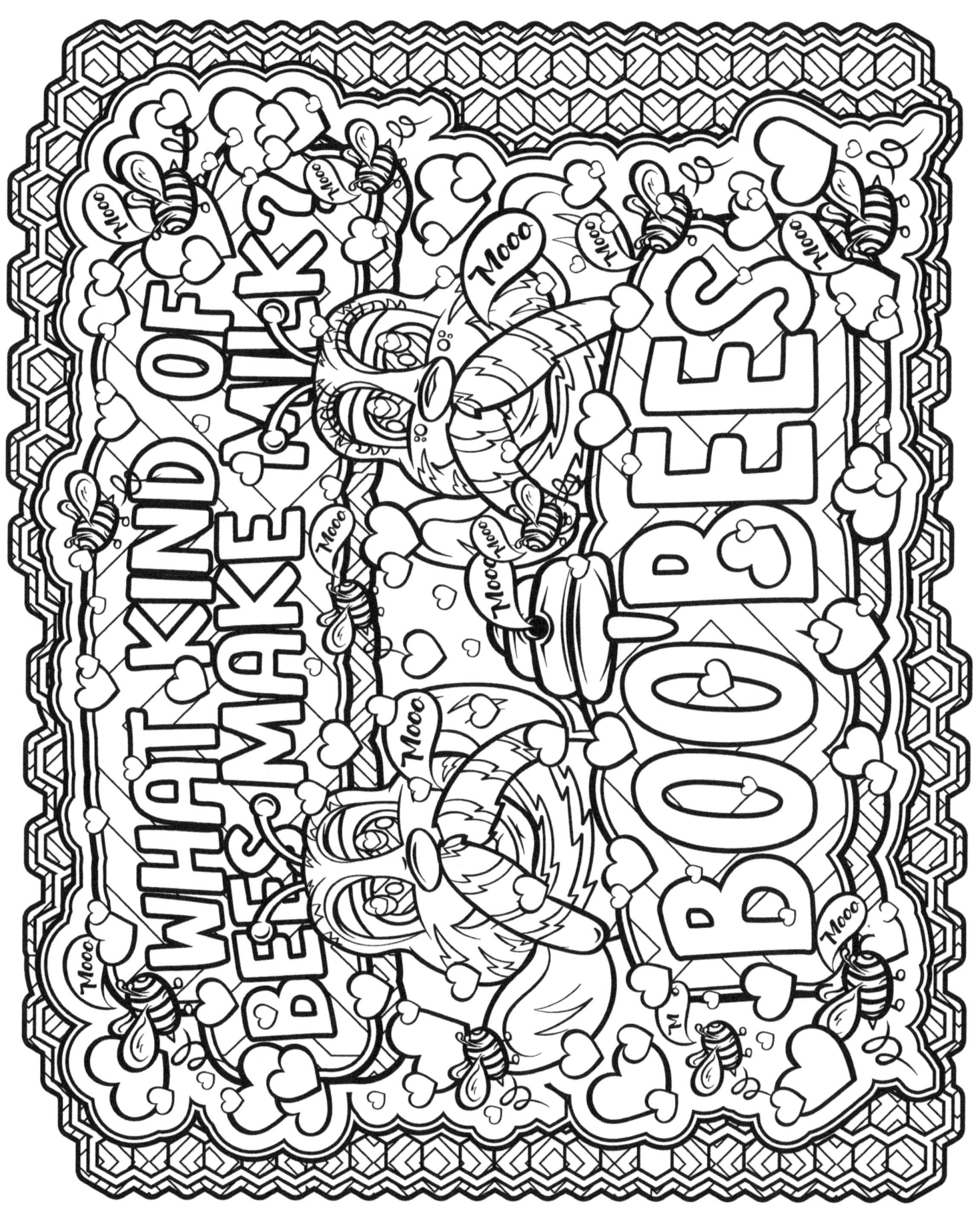

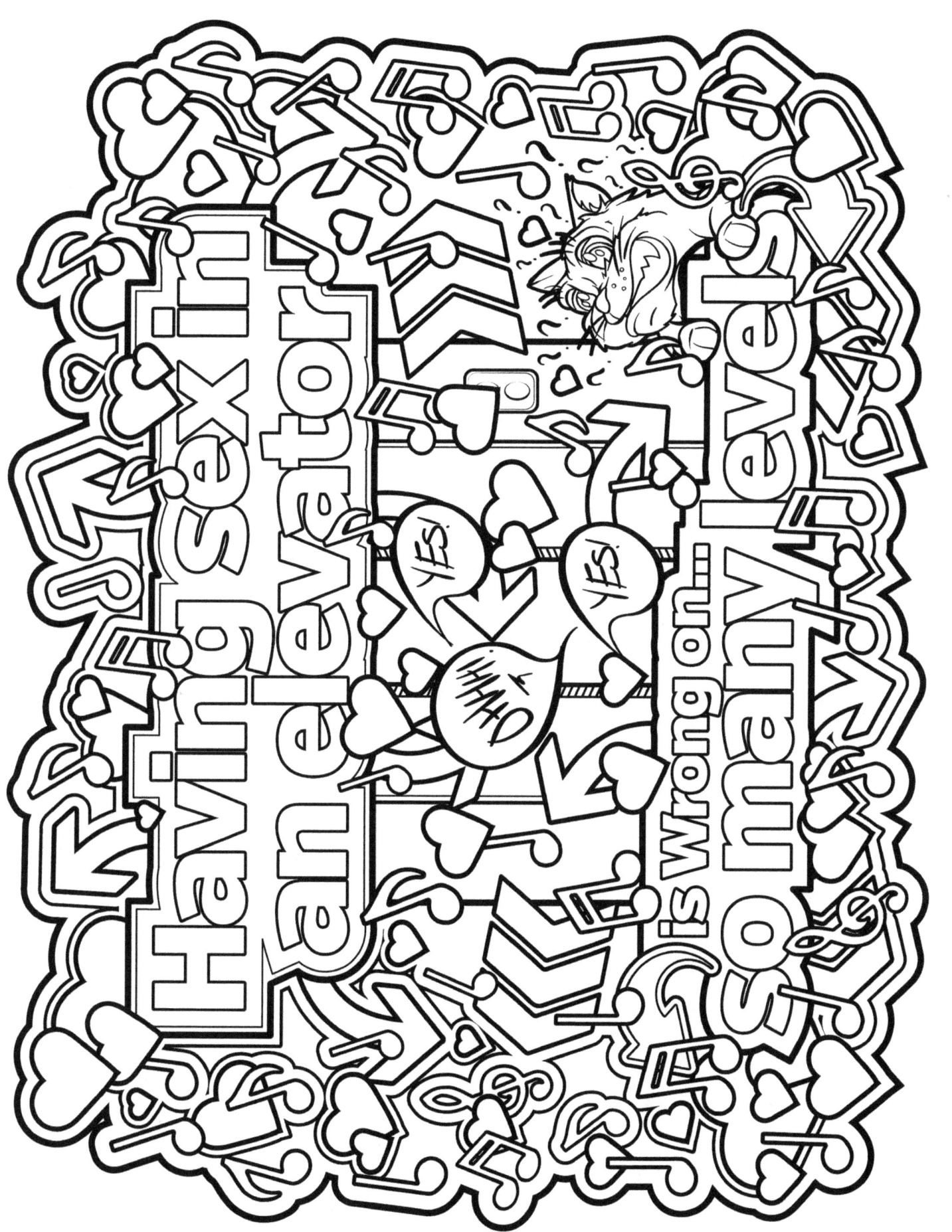

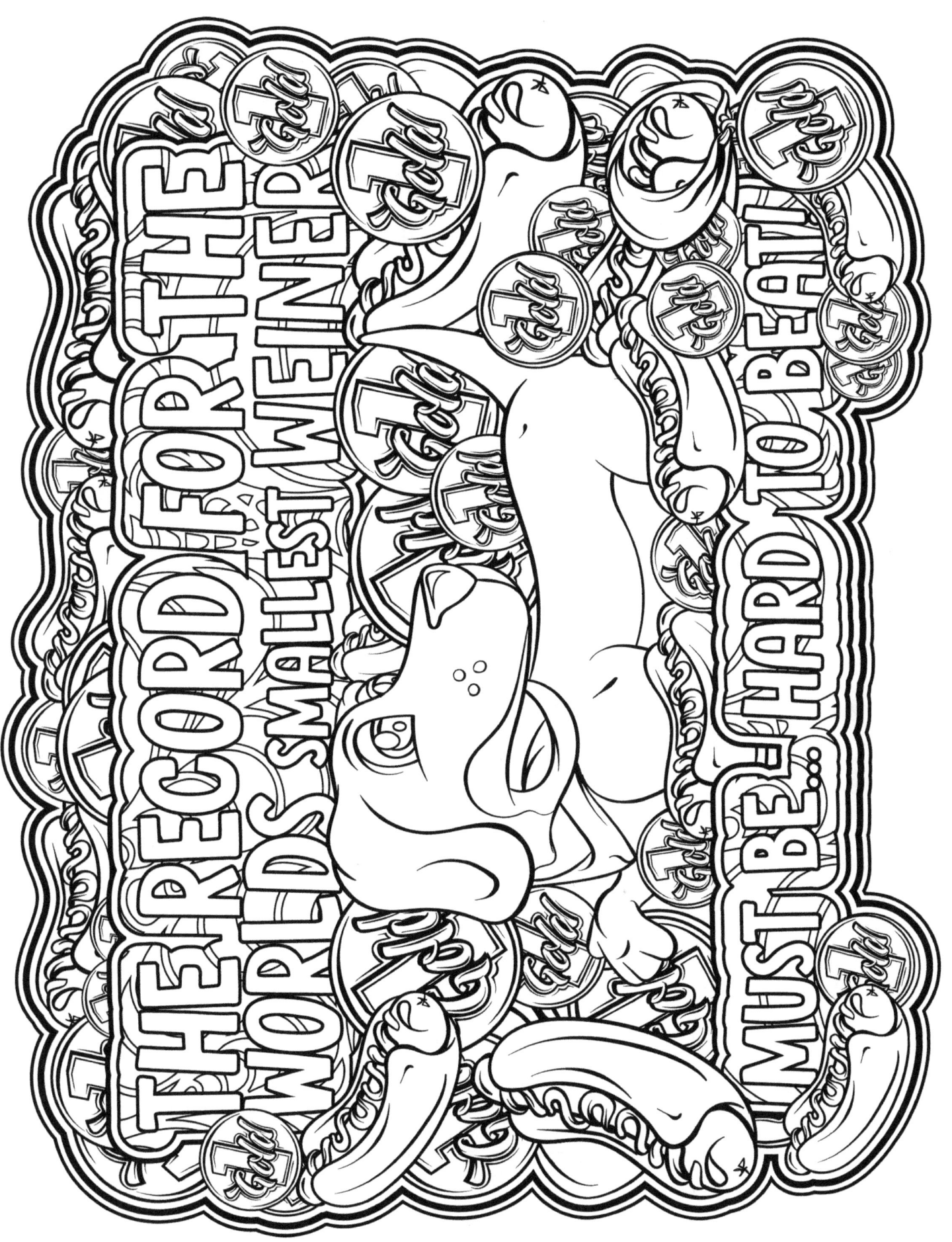

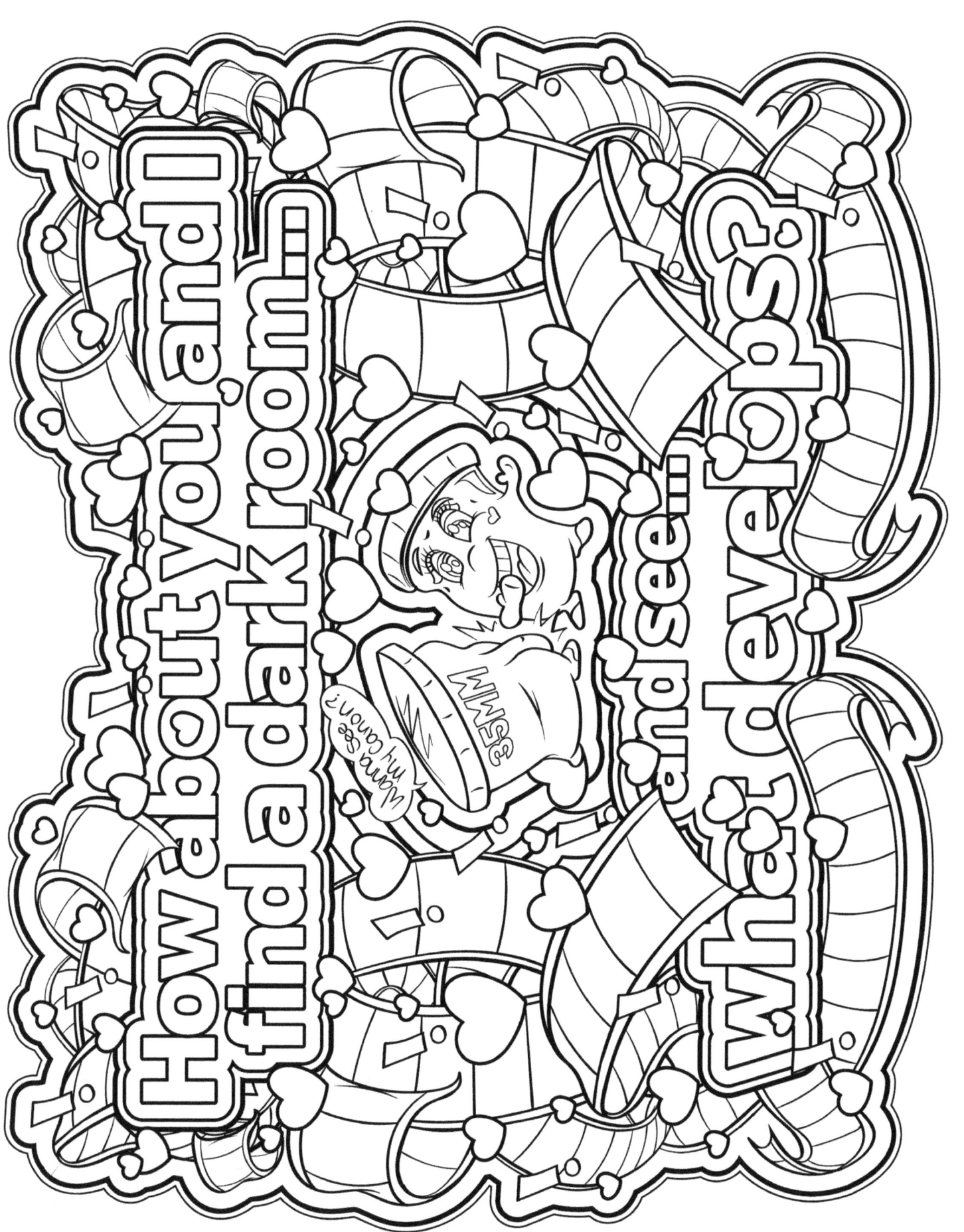

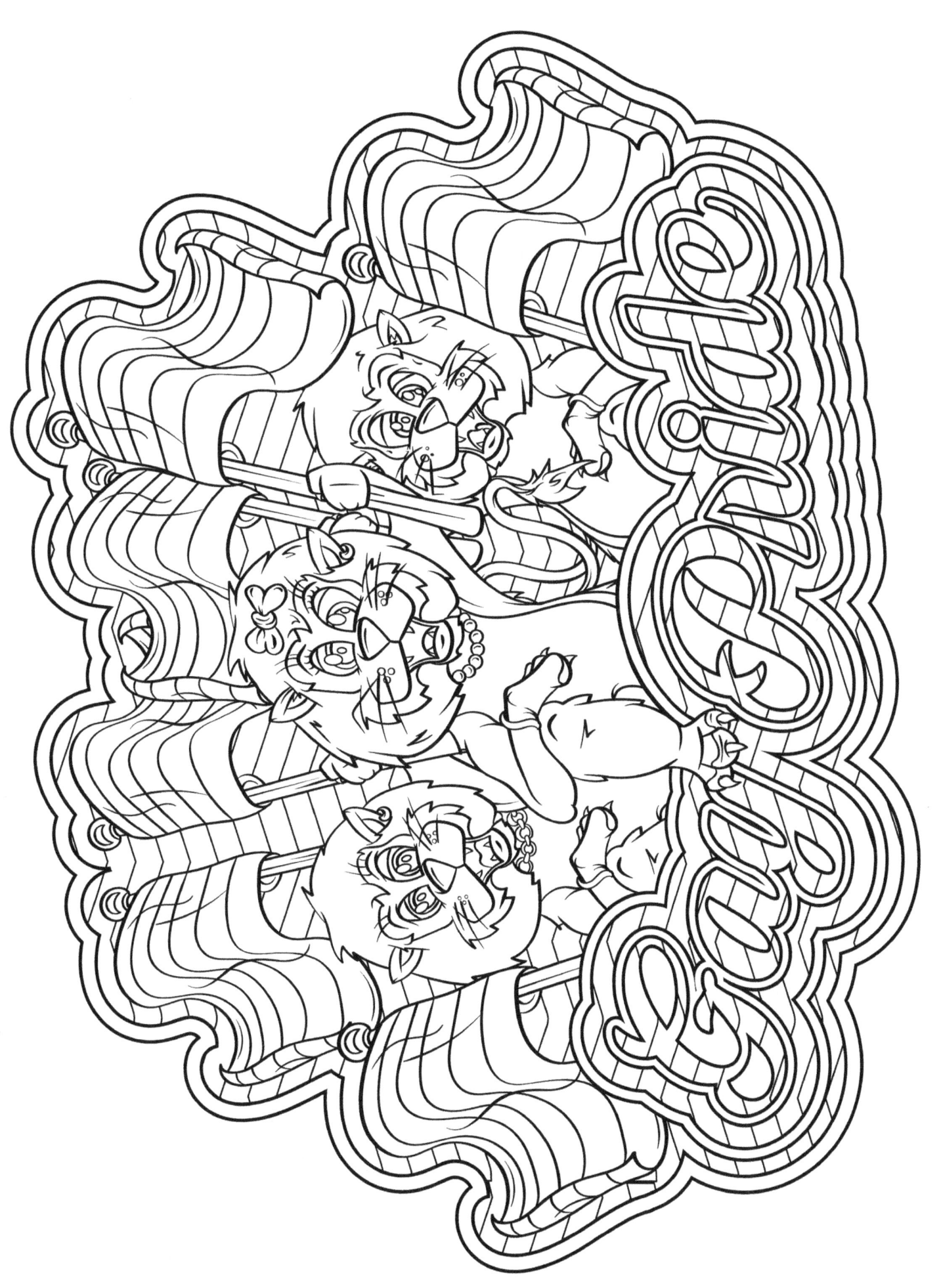

www.ingramcontent.com/pod-product-compliance
Lightning Source LLC
Chambersburg PA
CBHW081253040426
42453CB00014B/2405